Regarding *How to Talk about the Dead*

Jeff Newberry's one of our great poets of place—threading memory through local salt and sod to arrive at the universal. And his poems are prayers—quiet and resonant. Not so much tablets of wax as bees. Each poem one tiny traveler bringing home browsed and gleaned and bumped against flowers and lees. Inside Newberry's deft sensory weaves, the honey isn't in the lion's head: no, it's in our ears, on our eyes, and painted thick across our mouths. And always the bittersweet and the sweet intertwine. I finished this shining book and sat very still for a long time. Such is the rooted soaring you are in for. In *How to Talk about the Dead*, each walking stick is a dowsing rod.

—Abraham Smith, author of *Insomniac Sentinel & Dear Weirdo*

There is a progress situated fully in this new collection by Jeff Newberry beginning in the hard, green, at times bitter, realizations grown from childhood innocence and reprisals of the nuclear family set in home ground and waters of his native Gulf Coastal Florida and South Georgia. Questions of being continually surface in a determined self-examining poesis cast throughout this volume, where a natural ripening and softening occurs in the author's transcendence from fathered to father, fledgling to provider as he, with skilled hands and full-grown voice, traverses the soul's terrain. Herein you'll find some of the most miraculous tenderness ever committed to verse in a mortal suite devoted to his beloved just-born daughter, thread certain needles of realization beyond, and like whole life arrive at the gates of certain heaven wondering, as must we all, whether to go in.

—Sean Sexton, author of *Portals* and *May Darkness Restore.*

How to Talk about the Dead

Jeff Newberry's poems dwell on the borders between this world and one we sense but cannot see. But Newberry's poems let us know that the world we are barely aware of is as complicated and ultimately capricious as this one. "I'm faithful," Newberry claims in "The Bottom Fisher's Prayer," though he knows the existence he, and all of us, praise contains the "mayflies and gnat haze" he acknowledges just before this proclamation. Newberry also understands that in our dark times we need singers. "The Quarantine Haiku," a sequence written in early 2020, recalls the anxiety of those first months and we found our collective gaze turned inward and even sunlight was a portent. I could praise each poem in this collection, but the fact is that How to Talk About the Dead is the work of a poet in full possession of his powers. In language that is both spare and hunting, Newberry creates a world I want to spend more time in. Celebrate the strength of these poems and the man who wrote them.

—Al Maginnes, Author of *Fellow Survivors: New and Selected Poems*

How to Talk about the Dead

By
Jeff Newberry

REDHAWK
PUBLICATIONS

Copyright © 2024 by Jeff Newberry

All rights reserved. This book or parts thereof may not be reproduced in any form, stored in any retrieval system, or transmitted in any form by any means—electronic, mechanical, photocopy, recording, or otherwise—without prior written permission of the publisher, except as provided by United States of America copyright law. For permission requests, write to the publisher, at "Attention: Permissions Coordinator," at the address below.

Redhawk Publications
The Catawba Valley Community College Press
2550 US Hwy 70 SE
Hickory NC 28602

ISBN: 978-1-959346-35-7

Library of Congress Number: 2023951957

Printed in the United States of America

Layout and design by Chloe Sawyer
Cover image by Jeff Newberry
Author Photo by Joe Newberry

redhawkpublications.com

This is a work of fiction. Names, characters, and incidents either are products of the author's imagination or are used fictitiously. Any resemblance to actual events or persons, living or dead, is entirely coincidental.

This book is for my parents, Lang and Ginny.

Table of Contents

How to Talk about the Dead 11
On a Country Road in Calhoun County, Florida 12
Family Plot 13
The Dead Father Speaks 14
My Father's Shadow 15
About Disappointment 16
Days of 1986 17
Oysters 18
Elegy for Gulf County, Florida 19
How to Feel Patriotic in a Small Southern Town 21
Salt Marsh 23
The Bottom-Fisher's Prayer 24
Ode to the Mullet Fish 25
Controlled Burn 26
Ploughing 27
The Quarantine Haiku 29
Thomas Merton's Final Cleansing 37
Aubade on Black Rock Mountain 38
Imago Dei 39
Audubon 40
Lady of the Waters 41
Thankful 42
A Living Gallery 43
The Historian Tells Me About the Troubles 44
Richard Hugo in the Millvale Tavern 45
Treatise on Angels 46
Parable of the Moth 47
Satin Flowers in Graveyards 48
Discarded and Collected 49
Body Speaks 50
Annotations: An Elegy 51
The Late Poet 52
A Theology of Drought 52
Prayer after a Rare South Georgia Snow 53
What to Make of Air 55
Concept of Heaven 63
Kumquats 70
Acknowledgements 71
About the Author 73

*When it goes, 'tis like the Distance
On the look of Death –*
                    —Emily Dickinson

How to Talk about the Dead

Mention them by name only if you must.
Give them death's privacy. Let them be
no more than ghosted syllables, word-

shapes. Talk about their hands, the lined
palms, a lifeline that branches to anabranch
and disappears. Remember veined wrists,

purple and thin as pine saplings. Resist
the urge to turn those lines to words.
Remember instead aftershave and lilac

or alcohol and sweat, the presence they left
behind. Do not quote the dead. Their words
will not resurrect them. Instead, recall

only the timbre of a voice, how it brought
you here, now. You grunt and gasp at meaning,
a traveler in some foreign land, each ached

sentence a muted plea. The natives could
take you for dumb. They pity you instead.

On a Country Road in Calhoun County, Florida

My mother slows the car and says, "Look,"
and points to a woman on a stool
beside a bored Holstein swatting flies
with her tail, staring out at the pasture.

"I grew up doing that," she says and rolls
down the car window. The milking woman
smiles and waves. "I just wanted my boys
to see," my mother explains. "I grew up

on a farm. They've never even seen
a cow up close." "It's a different world now,"
the woman agrees. My brother and I stare,
the questions still-born on our ignorant

tongues. Outside, not twenty yards away,
a version of our mother—thin, young,
before her young dreams hardened
to the crust of middle-aged fears,

before split-shifts, before her daughter
came into the world to die a day later.
When we drive away, she stares
into the rearview mirror and will not
answer when we ask, "What's wrong?"

Family Plot

—Miller County, Georgia

We turn down a nearly invisible path
into a cotton field and follow the red dirt
deep into the rows where my cousin

shows me a fenced graveyard, the broken
gray stones worn and cracked with age,
their etched numbers and names faded.

I wander between markers and wonder
why my father—before he died—had never
so much as uttered a word about this place,

where my people molder beneath soil
they worked but never owned. "This is our
family," my cousin says and spreads her arms
to gesture all around. It is as close as I have
ever felt to them, buried in the ground.

The Dead Father Speaks

I am the dead father you have imagined
in countless poems and re-envisioned
in essays that find me quiet and pensive,
a stubbled face behind cigarette smoke,
a vision of a flannel shirt before I
step out the door for work each day.

I am the voice you hear when you fail,
the god you believe you can never please.

You don't know that in my vacant stares,
I was wondering why my guitar
stopped singing, why your mother—
who once held me tight between her legs—
became distant as a cormorant against a white
cloud in a picture I once tried to paint.
I failed at that, too, another thing unfinished.

My job? It was hell, even when I was
in charge, even when the bonus came
through, even when I came home,
wanting nothing more than to see you.

There were whole days you disappeared
into some vomit-colored television cartoon
I could never hope to cipher. When you
were a teen, I lost you for years
as you wandered through a dark tunnel
that would end when you emerged
transformed into some version of me
I could never be. When you noticed
my absence, I had just been there,
moments ago, waiting for you stop looking
for me and for you to see me instead.

My Father's Shadow

As a boy, I trailed behind on hot days,
hiding from the bright sun, secure

in the cool caul of his cast silhouette,
where I tried to fit my body into his mold,

my head into his place like a carnival
cut-out. There, I couldn't see his squint

or the red sheen on his forehead,
the sweat that ran from his hairline

down his cheeks like salted tears.
There, the burning heat stayed at bay.

I couldn't cast my own shadow there.
One day, I'd have to walk into the light

and bear the heat on my own. No more
hiding the lea of his ambling stone.

But then? I followed, walking on his back,
trying so hard to disappear into him.

About Disappointment

Early spring afternoon—
                              pre-bloom, the dogwoods spider
out like capillaries. Blackbirds scattershot in a peeled sky.

Their silhouettes dart like spent shells.
I've learned about disappointment by studying shadows,

how they grow with my body's tilt, break
left or right, according the sun's

charted angle. Don't look at it my mother warned
the year an eclipse darkened daylight to a dishwater dinge.

Believer I was, I stared at the sandy soil beneath my feet
and wondered how something hidden could blind me.

Days of 1986

In the evenings, my father drank
cheap beer, leaned forward in a cheap
chair, and watched beautiful men
beat each other to death on TV:
Boom Boom Mancini, Hit Man Hearns,
gladiators of sweat and blood and bile.

This was manhood: silent, aloof,
violent. My mother worked a split
shift and cleaned houses in between.

Once, our neighbor the hairdresser
lost her cat and two dogs killed it
while her daughter watched in horror.
My father slapped me when I cried
at the sight of blood and torn flesh.

The storms came each season,
and we fled north to relatives
I didn't know until home seemed safe
again. The roof never blew away.

After Hurricane Kate, a highway collapsed.
Trapped on a packed roadway, we sat silent
as a cop waved us by on a narrow
strip of land. My father drank
from a Budweiser can the police ignored.

My mother drove us home, where
the hairdresser sat on her porch,
drinking sweet tea and smiling.
She said, "I love this place. I really do."
That night, I kissed my father's stubbled
cheek and went to bed in a dark house,
silent in a power outage. He stank
of alcohol and sweat and love.

Oysters

Once, shuckers would crowd thirteen
or more on an ordered dozen,
crusted shells packed to the edge
of a tray, ice like mineral salts

between them, where they lay,
splayed, bivalves divers once
risked breath to bring to the air.
I've long heard tales of pearls

nestled deep in the gray-white
flesh but never felt one, hard
and round, on my tongue.
My father poured them from the shell

into his open throat and swallowed
them with drops of Crystal hot sauce
and long draughts of bitter beer.
We could shuck them ourselves,

but raw bars promised tray
after tray of Apalachicola's finest.
Now, the beds have shrunk in red
tides, the oysters fewer and fewer.

The prices make the raw bars stingy.
A dozen is just a dozen
as though just now, we've gleaned
their value, the pearl of their promise.

Elegy for Gulf County, Florida

A single water pipe sticks out of the sand
        where dried sea oats
sway. A silent highway stretches by,
        empty of summer traffic.
You said the sunset never changes,
        that the bay is the one true thing,
but the wind chimes echo anyway.
        The water tower still casts
a long, lone shadow over downtown,
        where the RCA shop and Badcock
stayed in business far too long.
        Now, it's all boarded windows
and cracked sidewalks. Even the mill's
        shuttered. Even the railroad
tracks are shaggy with grass.
        No one promised things wouldn't
change, but you seek it out anyway,
        the house you once knew,
held aloft by cinderblocks, the crawlspace
        beneath a storehouse of memories
like the summer a stray dog gave birth
        to a litter of puppies, who all
disappeared one by one and you mom
        said you couldn't have fed
them anyway. The house still stands,
        sure, but like everything else,
it's now what you remember.
        The door used to be bigger,
right? The window where you watched
        a yellow bus slow each morning
once framed your face. Now, it's gone,

        replaced with duct tape and cardboard.
What's left of this place is like sand
        on a beach, grains taken deep
into the ocean, swirled, twirled
        and brought back time and again.
The silt builds up, only to be taken back.
        No one finds sand dollars anymore.
The tourist shops took them all years ago.
        You can dig up fragments, though,
like periwinkles, like abalones,
        like scallop shells broken and sharpened.
Watch your hands when you dig.
        The tiny edges cut. They hurt.

How to Feel Patriotic in a Small Southern Town

It's not about the cherry bombs
tossed on the driveway while your old
man looks on, his can of Budweiser
the red and white to the blue smoke

curling out of his nose. It's not
about the Stars and Stripes Forever
Band on PBS or the celebrity posts
on Instagram or the chin-strap-bearded

boy who drives a Ford 4 X 4 through
your neighborhood, flying a rebel flag
the size of a king size sheet, and you
think of history class, where you learned

that some cultures celebrated virginity
on a wedding night when a newly-betrothed
bridegroom waved a blood-stained sheet
to a crowd of village onlookers who cheered

while inside the bride must have died,
her face flooding with the same blood,
the same color as this flapping flag,
As the truck rounds the corner yet again,

stereo blasting "Sweet Home Alabama,"
where George Wallace said segregation
now and forever. Somewhere south
of the highway, another community

like an unseen roommate must be
celebrating, too. Barbecue and family,
faces dark with worry as they scan
the street, where a truck may drive by,

a confederate flag waving in the night,
an intrusion they've learned to ignore.
A week ago, a police officer shot a teenager
jogging in a neighborhood this side

of the town. Wrong place. Wrong time.
Do I have to say it? Wrong color, too.
Just now, that pickup backfires, a sound
above the popping fireworks, the rocket's

red glare, the snap of American flags
in the evening breeze. One thing is certain:
it's not a gunshot, and if it is, it's not
meant for you. You're safe here. Safe and free.

Salt Marsh

Once, fishing in the saw grass, my pole held
high above, I sunk a leg to the thigh
into marsh and felt the earth hold me fast,

the rotted weeds and sand below a threat
to pull me deep and preserve me there,
where muck and shale turn shells to peat,

where fossils dissolve to become one
with the earth, reabsorbed. I could be
a bog body to unearth ages from now,

Specimen A in some archaeological
exploration, my deflated body now
corpus, evidence that the world changes

us but does not change. I twisted my foot
until it let me go and fell into the bracken
and swallowed sea water. Gasping, I took

great gulps of air and coughed, saved,
for the moment, from the spongy soil
that reclaims us all, that preserves us.

The Bottom-Fisher's Prayer

Lord, I don't need a cork
to know when the line is tight.
Just give me the muddy water's
ripple, the stillness

broken my something swift
deep beneath. I'm rooted
like a slash pine trunk,
sunk deep into this sandy soil.

Though mayflies and gnats
haze, I'm faithful.
Keep that bait in the water,
my father once taught me.

You never know the life
below. You never see
the channel cat's sleek
juke and turn—how he eyes

the cricket just to brush
against it, to dare the lip-sunk
hook, the tugging from above,
the promise to drag him into the light.

Ode to the Mullet Fish

Small-mouthed trash fish no one
wants to eat save the locals
who know your sweet, oily meat,

my mother used to get you free
from the fishery down by the canal,
who threw in your spiny backbone

and clotted roe free. When my father
threw his cast net into the bay,
the weights took it low, where you

ran, bottom feeders like all of us.
Forty years later, I tried to order
you, crisp and fried, in a Georgia

restaurant, three hours from the bay
we once called home. The flesh tasted
strong and briny. I'd forgotten. Too

far from the sea, you're quick to rot.
You need the salt to extend your life,
to hold the taste inside, just like me.

Controlled Burn

They're burning away undergrowth,
the pine and palm scrub, felled
saplings and fallen limbs and vines
that turn to mulch on the forest floor.

Men have formed a sort-of line
along this stretch of woods. Hard hats
and orange vests, they stand in the smoke,
shovels ready to suffocate an errant spark.

I smell woodsmoke for days after, a charred
stench that drags me from my thoughts
of the past, movies I replay in my mind,
the images that keep coming back

like some perennial growth, evergreen
made new with each year, a rooted
story that feeds my mind's hard, wooden
resolve. I should burn it off, too,

but it feels dishonest, shoveling dirt
on the past, as though the embers
wouldn't continue to glow, as though
the burning wouldn't make it all new again.

Ploughing
After Seamus Heaney

He had no mule (I'm told),
so my grandfather pushed a plough
into the red Georgia clay,
turning up rows for planting,
where he sowed cotton and peanuts
he sold to provide for the family.

My mother says he kept even
rows, straight as the razor
he used to shave each day.
He could squint in 90-degree sun
And leave plough lines
scored and crisp, evenly split,
long, drawn lines on the earth.

My days are not like his. I see lines
of prose and poems in dusty volumes
and cough and gag in peanut dust.
My nights find me awake and sure
that no matter what I do,
I'll never turn the earth like him.

So, I push a pen into this page,
though I differ from him
in time and age. Still, I like
to watch the ink unfurl
like rows of dark, black earth,
the good soil, where life takes root.

The Quarantine Haiku

Trout dimple the lake's
morning sheen as we drop lines
into their wet kiss.

*

The hush of rain:
A dialect of silence
No one knows to speak.

*

Dawn. The world inhales.
The day is dewy and wet
as a newborn child.

Sunlight blades across
the blue, severing the night
from day's bright promise.

*

Storm-bowed loblollies
lift from the ground, roots earth-
dark, still drinking life.

*

At dusk, a wren calls,
perched on a telephone line
we no longer use.

A log truck rumbles
down a rural road, flat bed
packed with spring-cut pines.

*

Springtime confetti:
a paper plate's white shards
in a mower's wake.

*

On the last cool day
of spring, unused cords of wood
recall a warm autumn.

Reading on the porch,
he nods toward sleep, just like
the old man he's become.

*

An afternoon for wine
and conversation. Instead,
the bistro's empty.

*

The afternoon's cool
breeze won't chase away the gnat
buzzing in my ear.

Wading out beneath
gray skies, he throws a cast net.
It blooms like a cloud.

*

My son's voice echoes
across the yard like the years
that separate us.

*

Cool dirt in the dark
alley as he walks home from
Granny's—Georgia dusk.

This colorless dawn,
a bluebird pecks in gray grass
and ruffles its feathers.

*

An irrigation
spigot stands spindly and still
In an empty field.

*

An afternoon sun
Blazes, cupped in the palm
Of a cloudless sky.

*

The path opens up
To a cotton field, the bolls
Heavy with sunlight.

Thomas Merton's Final Cleansing

The water is a metaphor, washing
away sins, yes, but more—meditative
might be the word. All dirt and dead cells,
It sluices down his neck and pools

between his feet. The body reborn
watches the body slough off another skin
suit. Lizard-like, he thinks, we're creatures
who seek sun but need water to survive.

This story sustains: that life is not
dress rehearsal for eternity, that each
moment is one of Blake's grains of sand.
In Thailand, the winds come, humid,

smelling of the sea to which we all
return. Clean, he turns off the faucet,
step up on the tub's edge, and marvels
at the foot's veined architecture, thinks

of providence, how we're all pulled
toward a divine center of gravity, as he
is here, now, in this moment. He steps
out into the breeze of an electric fan.

Aubade on Black Rock Mountain

A morning chill grips the cabin, reminds
me that in the end, I'm bone and body,
meat on a frame. What can die can rot.
The pelt drying outside had been
a six-point yesterday morning. Even
plant matter mulches. Roots drink
from the rot. I've boiled coffee and sip
the black, grit my teeth against the morning
wind. An old man at church told me
some Native American tribes imagined
hell an endless tundra of frozen soil.
No food, no nothing. It was their
worst nightmare. Hell, then, must be
the worst we can imagine. On this lonely
mountain, I can imagine anything.
Outside, I study last night's campfire
ashes, consider the sweet gum and pines
consumed by fire. I sat up late looking
for patterns in the sky. Ancient sailors
did the same, I've read–traced meaning
into the stars' chaos. Only one remains fixed,
though, the North Star, while the rest whirled
like the fiery wheels Van Gogh saw. I kneel
now by the fire pit and run my fingers
through ashes, snatch my hand away.
Somewhere in the gray, a spark remains.

Imago Dei

When at last they dig our bones up
in some shattered city, they'll find bullets
and think them tiny statues, shaped

in temples by reverent hands. Offered up
to now-silent gods. They'll see our rotund
forms in grained photographs and imagine

us crafting tiny version of ourselves.
Like all ancients, a professor will say,
they built gods in the form of themselves.

Someone will pity us. Some will scorn.
They'll find the pistols, too, the guns
and rifles, their sleek barrels now rust-

speckled, riddled with holes that sunlight
sieves through and shines on the ruins.

Audubon

They called not in voices
but symbols I scried revealed
to me in more than a calling—
Call it life's work. Call it art.

Call it the bone-deep belief
that all should see the plumed
darts in these nascent skies.

To sketch a thing is to love it
the way a lover holds a hand,
tracing the lines fortune tellers

read to forecast the length
and breadth of our piteous lives,
as we stumble about, earth-bound,

eyes always up, seeking what?
Escape? Or something better still—
confirmation that it's possible

even as a sparrow falls to the ground.

Lady of the Waters
—Louisiana Heron by James Audubon (1834)

Crooked tree trunks resist the frame's order.
They rise from swamp water like the spindled
arms of some chthonic creature
pulled from the shadows concealed
in the mud of our unconscious.

In the foreground, she looks behind, long neck
and thin legs rendered in a swept stroke
I imagine he drew with studied elegance,
resisting a quick flourish. Avian,
his hands moved like tiny white birds.

No kinetic frenzy on canvas, this life
study reveals intent in color, a rendered
ancestor of lizards that once tread
an earth not so different from the swamped
background. Now, a burst of purple and blue,
white filigree, feet so light they don't leave
imprints in sand. The colors pull the eyes
and resolve the muddy past, where the heron
could take flight, were it real, to escape.

Thankful

Dear birds, whose names I do
not know, forgive me for not

taking the time to learn: wren,
sparrow, mourning dove, finch.

Like your song, your names note
and quarter note on my tongue.

I try to imitate you, but my songs
fail, as they often do. Forgive me

for wanting that trill in my throat.
Forgive me for not just listening,

for turning your music into my own.

A Living Gallery

An egret lands on the deck
and for a moment, it's art,
a painting I once saw walled

between an ibis and gull
nn a museum show: Avians
Of the Southeast. No mix

and smear on a palette,
the bird hitches its head
and takes a hitching step

before its wings stretch
and aloft, it takes to the sky.
Earthbound, I try to lock

this memory in place, a gallery
I visit when I remember the way—
the sudden, strange way—

the world can still shock me,
a boy who stares at his reflection
and swears he saw it wink.

The Historian Tells Me About the Troubles
—For Hubert Van Tuyll

By the shore in Dungarven, you speak
of home and its problems, the sheared
and trimmed confetti we call history
while we eat fish and chips wrapped

in phony newspaper print the restaurant
bought (I assume) to ensure some notion
of tradition. You tell me this old country
has seen its problems, too, that decades

pass like cards in a dealer's nimble hands.
No one knows the hand until the play.
You mean to comfort. I see the suicide
King, dealt to me by a faceless man

who does not know my name. A poet
once called history a gyre, a seer
who unfolded visions from the variegated
striations of dreams. "Who's to say?"

you wonder aloud. "About what?"
I want to reply. My mouth full of flesh,
I mumble what might be assent. Turning
and turning west toward home, I stare

at a single bird, slouching to the east.

Richard Hugo in the Millvale Tavern
—For Cody Smith

His students would symbol the mounted goat head
behind the bar, so he sips bourbon to consider
black and brown striations in a cedar floor.
Two nights ago, weather broke in the west,
lightning walked across a veined sky,
rain fell like the last secret you spill in hell.
Barbara couldn't sleep, but he'd been up, pleased
to hear the rattled rhythm. Alone, he

nodded to sleep when thunder deafened
the home's closets and hallways. Close up,
whiskey takes the tinge of bilge water.
That's a poem, sure, but so is this hard seat,
these hard-faced men, the bright best girls
now foot-tapping wives who walk floors
and the children sleeping in cool, open rooms.

At last the drunk arrives and shakes off
his hat and hails the fellas. Dick would buy him
a drink if the old man would take it.
The highball's bottom appears like a spyglass
and he studies some Indian's initials
etched into old wood. He nods another drink,
so the barkeep pours. Barbara's worried
because a bear broke into the garage
their second week here. She doesn't know
that's the most beautiful thing that's happened.
His students are right. There's a metaphor here.

Treatise on Angels

I once thought them God's celestial warriors,
aglow in holy white, their wings
edged as a razor, their blazing eyes
without pupils, inscrutable as glass.
Soldiers in an eternal war,
they saw humanity deluded and ignorant,
cut off and safe in the fallen world.

Others have pictured Rubenesque children,
hands clasped together in prayer,
their lamb's hair perfect and curled
beneath a halo shining holy light.

In movies, they've been God's messengers,
go-betweens, agents of fate—
heaven's errand boys quick with words
of wisdom and a solemn head nod
to the sky, a mention of The Big Guy.

Seraphim, cherubim, inhuman,
they appear as we seek them:
in crosses of fire, in the late light
of a father's funeral or brilliant, luminous,
and embossed on a greeting card
purchased to say, "I'm sorry for your loss."

They look out from where we see
them, filled with a knowledge
of eternity, their sad eyes longing,
their faces familiar—
almost, but not quite human.

Parable of the Moth

When he opens the front door,
a moth follows. Speckled, the color
of a forest floor, it dives and rises,

settles in a corner and stays, still
and silent. He could swat it, yes,
but wants to pick at it like a problem

or scab and study what lies beneath
the worry. Once, as a child, he woke
convinced his parents were dead

and would not allow himself to check
their beds. What if they were gone?
He sat on the cool carpet all night

until the door opened, and lamp light
spilled on him. He turned toward his father,
who might have been dead an hour ago,

and could not say why he still felt fear.
He tries to rest on the easy chair,
a long day behind him. It draws

his eyes, an uneasy glance
at this meaningless, harmless thing,
drawn inside by the promise of light.

Satin Flowers in Graveyards

These die, too. In spring storms of hail and wind, in the sun's relentless burn. Even fake flowers fade. The florist downtown keeps a stock of funeral-ready banners and bouquets: In Remembrance, RIP, crepe crosses—the rented grief you see after grave-side services when only the tent remains. Somewhere, the left behind eat cold fried chicken and pretend that everything tastes the same.

My aunt set fake bouquets by my father's and uncle's graves for years and years before death came for her, too. I miss the Styrofoam-bottomed plastic vases that once littered the family plot. No one puts flowers there anymore. When I stand over these plain gray slabs, grass grows up to the edge. I left a framed poem at my father's grave once. A week later, the rain had bleached the paper white as though I'd never written a word.

Discarded and Collected

When I see a person stop, kneel,
and take another's discarded

trash from the sidewalk and drop
it in a nearby garbage can, all

without breaking their stride,
I stop and consider all the refuse

I've ignored in my life and all
the people who have come behind me

to take a quick knee and gather
up the things I didn't throw away.

Body Speaks
—*After Ira Sukrungruang*

Body says "feed me" though body says "I hurt."
Body says "salt," says "sugar,"
says "You look like a horse's hind quarters."
Body says "Wait, one day you'll be beautiful."
Body says, "You lost five pounds."
Body gains five and five more again.
Body says, "Tilt your head just right.
No one will see this double chin."
Body forgets and sees self in mirrors
and remembers: "I am fat. I am body alone."
Body says "embarrassment," says "fat boy,"
says "Big 'un" like the tenth grade coach
who said, "You're bigger than anything
they have at Sea World." Body dies
thinking of the girl who wouldn't touch
body in college, who said it wasn't body,
but body knows better. Body is not sexual.
Body is asexual. Body is a fleshy suit.
Body is a machine of narrowed veins
and a heart pumping like a steam engine.
Body is "obese." Body is "morbidly obese."
Body fears doctors, who tap charts, suck teeth
and say, "You need to lose a lot of weight.
This is all going to catch up with you soon."
Body fears loss so Body consumes more.
Body doubles down. Body opts for supersize.
Body takes the refill. Body sinks down,
worn, spent, so tired of all this weight.

Annotations: An Elegy
—*For Thomas Sunday (1967-2020)*

I still have an old copy of Huck Finn,
dog-eared and faded, margins scratched
in your hand, next to a Dylan biography
and a few volumes of Faulkner you loaned
me years ago. Lately, I've been turning
my head and seeing you—not you,
not quite. Youness. The quality of your
being, etched into the corner of my vision.

Once we could have entire conversations
in movie lines. Pacino. Tarantino. Sam Jackson
in a breakfast café, leaned over uneaten eggs,
swearing to walk the earth like Kane.
We could talk in music, too, like nights
we traded songs and drank cheap beer
because we were young and made poetic
every small, insignificant thing in our lives.

My children repeat things I say, as I
repeat things my father said, my mother said.
My wife reminds me, "That's what you said,"
when I forget what I claimed I would do.

This afternoon, the ghost moon in a bright
sky made me think of the night to come.
My old friend, we once shared a star
as we drank the last of a bottle of bourbon.
The ancients made the sky a narrative,
put their heroes there to have a thing
to aspire to, an imagined life beyond this.
We make constellations of our lives,
connecting events to draw pictures
we name to give meaning, an empty beauty
that tells us together, we are alone.

The Late Poet

At the reading, the famous poet
holds his book less like a sacred
tome I've marked up like a cave
wall and more like a phonebook,

a list of names and places he can't
remember. After, in line, I offer
my copy for his signature and pray
he understands the way his words

have scored into my mind. He does
not make eye contact and passes
it back. I move for the next in line.
When he dies a month later, I want

to make this moment sacred. Take
a lesson like a soothsayer's rhyme.
Alone with his book, I turn a familiar
page. Look at the clock—at the time.

A Theology of Drought

No rain for a month. The crops die
in the parched loam, tomatoes
dried up, squash turned to mush.

We pray. The clouds drift east
like dreams we know better than chase.

"The real tragedy's the soil,"
an old timer says at the Northside Cafe
one morning, black coffee steaming
from his third cup. "You can see
what's dying if you look, but down
deep—there's the real problem."

We all grunt to agree. Even if
the weather turns, the earth drying.

What you don't see can kill you,
my father once said, meaning snakes
curled behind fallen logs. The earth

once cried for Abel's blood.
It's been thirsty ever since.

Prayer after a Rare South Georgia Snow

Call the cold apocalyptic. Unseasonable.
                    A vortex of arctic chance.

Call it climate change or End of Days.
                    Call them unfortunate, those packed

in a stalled school bus on I-75.
                    The children who once prayed

for a snow day watch the world freeze.
                    Call black ice natural,

the lines of cars and trucks inevitable.
                    Call us unprepared.

Call frozen top soil a tragedy.
                    Dismiss our pleas with platitudes.

But hear, oh hear our words
                    feathering from frosted lips,

voices rising to a sky   silent as snow.

What to Make of Air

Out of the mocking-bird's throat, the musical shuttle. –Whitman

i.

In the NICU, the hours are like the breath
you take before you speak, but held

in place by the burden of a secret you can't tell.
Air: endless, essential, the oxygen forced

through your daughter's thin cannula.
Three days old with a three-inch scar

on her back, stitched and bandaged.
The neurosurgeon said *She's a good case,*

the best I've ever seen. You ask
what good case means in the language

of Spina Bifida. He opens his mouth
as though to speak, and you can picture

the words gathering in his shuttled throat,
ready to weave themselves into existence.

ii.

Each time the baby takes a breath,
you stare at your sleeping girl,

her bird bones. Her bird-like breast
rising and falling, rising and falling.

The nurse who taught you pediatric
CPR said We have this much room

to breathe and held up a pen you
might use to write a poem or a song.

iii.

The first thing new singers learn:
breathe. Control the way air passes

the lips and expands the diaphragm.
Regulate the oxygen you need

to vibrate a tone or word. To sustain—
a word you said last night in a quick

drowsy prayer, the Our Fathers
constant as you slipped away.

How can I sustain it? you thought
to or at God, whose angels sing

but never want for air. They dance
on clouds, you learned as a child,

their feet never touching this fallen
earth. You were taught God watched

his son die. How to sustain it?
You'd like to take your own child

up into your arms and sing Hush
little baby, don't say a word. Daddy's

gonna buy you a mockingbird.

iv.

The tubes and wires and alarms
hold her fast. Her body is as frail

as the glass a soprano can shatter.
In the NICU, her Plexiglass bed

does not crack. You count her fingers
that may one day snap to a rhythm

you teach her. You count her breaths.
You think of music rests and listen

to the neighbor baby's screams
and the whirring machines that keep

her alive. You match your breathing
to your daughter's and watch her mouth

move without sound. You mouth
nursery rhymes and imagine her voice.

You wonder how breath becomes song.

v.

No one comes some days. Other days,
the nurses swoop in, a white-clad choir

who tap tablets with gloved fingers
as though playing an alien instrument.

To speak would be to acknowledge them—
to acknowledge this liminal space

between the thought of your daughter
and the idea of her, somehow walking

out on her own. That fantasy won't
even become pictures in your mind.

You hum tunes instead and say hmmm....
when the nurses ask you how you feel.

vi.

One day, you think, you will write
about this. Write. Write. How trite,

the hurt daughter poem. The poem that turns
her month here into neat lines on white

paper. The poem that one might mouth
or hear only in the mind. The poem

that can't find the language that lies
just beyond the grasp of metaphor.

A baby wired to a machine that breathes.
How dare you? you think. How dare

you stoop to art to make this all make
sense. Remember, poesis is to make.

vii.

It's midnight when you awaken in the hard chair,
a magazine butterflied on your chest,

an empty cup of machine-brewed coffee
spilled down your pants, cold and damp.

The pulse monitor goes up and down in silent
whole notes. It matches a song you heard

a long time ago, something you used to sing
when you drove along a coastal highway,

the window down, the wind in your face
smelling of pine trees and salt water and life.

viii.

Now, she's awake, staring out the glass cube
at you, her tiny bird eyes blue, filled with light.

You tap the side of her bed. You tap tap tap
the tune, "Hush little baby, don't you cry."

It's crying you want. Crying you need.
Her cry could show you how much life

is coiled inside her, how much she needs to say.
Her fingers uncurl. She exhales, alive.

Conceptions of Heaven

i.

I have dreams of an isolated cabin
by a pond where fish dimple the water.
Mountains in the distance. A faded
wooden dock, where I stand to behold
the silence. I drink coffee and never
tire. All day, alone. At night, no dreams.

ii.

My family has gathered in my dreams.
A long table lined with food. A cabin
filled with joyous song. The party never
seems to end. I drink wine and water.
My father smiles, and the child I hold
will not age to a hazy memory, faded.

iii.

My Baptist childhood said I was fated
to float on a cloud with a harp, a dream
the preacher taught me how to hold
in my mind, cupped like a match in a cabin,
a place so dry it could go up. No water
can douse the fire, which burns forever.

iv.

The soul emerges into some gray never.
No color. No shadows. Just a gray, faded
landscape. No horizon. No fire. No water.
Nothing to sense, so, then, nothing to dream.
Here, there's no land to build your cabin.
Here, you've only got forever to behold.

v.

My dead father is teaching me a song. He holds
a guitar, seeking the right chords. I've never
seen him play. Once, we stayed in a cabin
to fish for a week and didn't speak. I waded
out to avoid him, ignored him to catch bream.
Now, he sings in a voice like river water.

vi.

If the streets are paved with gold, is the water
liquid silver? If the harps all the angels hold
never cease, wouldn't I want to just scream?
The Gates of Heaven are locked. No one's ever
scaled the walls to break in. I must be fated
to live eternity alone, isolated in some cabin.

vii.

Some nights, I dream of endless water.
Other nights, I behold cabin after empty cabin.
My mind is empty as slate. The images fade.

Kumquats

—For Lang Newberry (1939-1990)

It looked like a stunted orange tree
in our backyard, the waxy leaves
shining in sunlight, glistening after rain,
tiny fruit the size of thumb's fat tip.

My father picked them by the bowl
and ate them at the kitchen table.
Once, I popped one into my mouth,
the bite so sour tears burned my eyes,

the taste so sharp I couldn't see
how he chewed them with a smile.
My thoughts of him have been
like that: the tart sting that sears

the tongue and blurs my vision,
the fruit I pick although I know
it will sour my mouth. I take a bite
because I like to taste the burn.

Acknowledgements

Versions of these poems have appeared in the following publications:

Book of Matches
Connotations: An Online Artifact
Crab Orchard Review
Columbia Review
Cumberland River Review
Journal of American Poetry
Main Street Rag
North American Review
Relief: A Journal of Arts and Faith
South Florida Poetry Journal
The Lake
The Laurel Review
The MacGuffin

Many thanks to the editors who gave my work a chance. Thank you, too, to Justin Evans, Cody Smith, Michael Meyerhoffer, Al Maginnes, Jeff Hardin, Gary McDowell, John Gallaher, Jim Clarke, Justin Hamm, Sîan Griffiths, Ed Pavlic, Sean Sexton, Patti Smith, Rick Campbell and others who read many versions of these poems. Your support, friendship, and encouragement mean everything to me.

About the Author

Jeff Newberry is an essayist, novelist, and poet. His writing has been published in a wide variety of print and online journals, including *Apalachee Review*, *Brevity: Concise Nonfiction*, *The MacGuffin*, *Memorious*, *North American Review*, *Southeast Review*, *South Florida Poetry Review*, *Sweet*, and others. His chapbook, *A Visible Sign*, was a nominee for the Conference on Christianity and Literature's Book of the Year. His other publications include a collection of poetry *(Brackish)*, a collaborative manuscript with the poet Justin Evans *(Cross Country)*, and a novel *(A Stairway to the Sea)*. He teaches in the Writing and Communication Program at Abraham Baldwin Agricultural College in Tifton, Georgia.

www.ingramcontent.com/pod-product-compliance
Lightning Source LLC
Chambersburg PA
CBHW021025090426
42738CB00007B/906